Introduction

I've created hundreds of stuffed animals in my years as a sewing pattern designer. Typically I spend several hours perfecting the shape of an animal's body—getting just the right curve for a cat's back or the perfect stance for a horse. When it came to designing the toys in this book, however, the process was different and it was quite a wonderful change.

Every one of these puzzle balls is essentially the same in its body shape. Individual segments are sewn together into rings, which then interlock to form a ball that can be assembled and disassembled. Each body is a sphere.

The simplicity and repetition of the ball shape allowed me to focus on accentuating the essential features of each animal: the head, the tail, the ear and the legs. It also required me to choose distinctive fleece fabrics that would make the balls lively and the animals recognizable.

I wish to thank my husband, Charlie, and my three daughters—Roxanne, Stella and Josephine—for your love and encouragement.

I hope you enjoy the clever way these toys are designed, and I hope the children you make them for delight in taking them apart and puzzling them back together again.

Happy sewing,

Abby Glassenberg

Sew & Play Puzzle Ball Animals was inspired by Amamani Puzzle Balls, *a best-selling crochet book by Dedri Uys. We would like to express to Dedri a special thanks for creating an adorable set of crocheted puzzle ball animals, and then allowing us to offer a similar collection made with fleece.*

Meet the Designer

Abby Glassenberg creates unique patterns for stuffed animals from her home studio in Wellesley, Mass. Since 2005 she has shared her creations and ideas on design, technique and the online culture of craft through her blog www.whileshenaps.com and the *While She Naps* podcast.

Abby has a master's degree in education from Harvard and taught middle school social studies in Mississippi and Massachusetts before becoming a textile artist and the mother of three girls. Today Abby enjoys teaching people how to sew and opening their eyes to the joy of designing their own stuffed animals.

Table of Contents

Need assembly help?
Video Tutorial
AVAILABLE AT
ANNIESCRAFTSTORE.COM

Getting Started

Basic Tools

You will need some of the basic hand- and machine-sewing tools listed in Basic Sewing Supplies & Equipment and the following specific tools and materials to make your puzzle ball toys (Photo 1):

Photo 1

- 100% polyester thread
- Buttonhole twist or topstitch thread
- Chalk
- Fabric marker with water-soluble or air-soluble ink
- Ballpoint awl
- Embroidery needle
- Embroidery floss
- No. 8 pearl cotton
- Embroidery scissors
- 8mm safety eyes with washers

Basic Sewing Supplies & Equipment

- *Sewing machine in good working order*
- *Matching all-purpose thread*
- *Hand-sewing needles and thimble*
- *Straight pins and pincushion*
- *Seam ripper*
- *Removable fabric markers or tailor's chalk*
- *Measuring tools*
- *Pattern tracing paper or cloth*
- *Point turner*
- *Dry/steam iron, ironing board and press cloths*
- *Scissors and shears*

Patterns Included

We have used industry standard markings on the patterns included in this book to make them easy to use. Each pattern includes a ¼-inch seam allowance and straight-grain line as well as other pattern marks to make construction easier.

Patterns are included at full size. Make patterns by tracing the included patterns onto pattern tracing paper or tissue paper.

Be sure to transfer all markings from the included pattern.

Be aware that some of the patterns will be used for multiple animals. For example, the Lion, Giraffe and Elephant share the same tail pattern pieces. The Cap, Wedge, Foot Pad and Leg patterns are used to make all the leg segments and rings.

Sewing With Fleece

Made from 100 percent polyester fibers, fleece is a totally synthetic fiber first developed in the late 1970s. Its popularity stems from several appealing properties. Fleece is warm, soft, machine washable and comes in lots of bright colors, making it a wonderful fabric for toys.

If you've never sewn with fleece before it can be a bit intimidating because it's rather thick and stretchy, but with a few tips, you'll see that fleece is actually very forgiving and easy to sew with.

Cutting Fleece

Most fleece has two distinct sides: a smooth one and a textured one as shown in Photo 2. When you gently pull the fabric along the cross grain it will curl toward the wrong or smooth side which indicates that the textured side is the right side.

Photo 2

Right side of fleece. Wrong side of fleece.

It is easier to cut small toy pattern pieces from a single layer of fabric. Lay out the fabric right side up and position pattern pieces with the printed side up. If two of the same piece are needed and the second

is to be reversed, position the pattern upside down or reversed and cut a second piece. Specific cutting instructions are given on each pattern.

Like all fabrics, fleece does have a straight grain. Lengthwise grain is parallel to the selvages, and cross-wise grain is perpendicular to the selvages. Line up straight-grain arrows on the patterns parallel to the fabric's selvage.

Stitching Fleece

The pattern pieces for the puzzle balls are relatively small and tend to have several curves. Pinning every ¼ inch will hold the layers securely while you sew (Photo 3). When attaching a part such as an ear or antenna, hand-baste it in place before machine sewing.

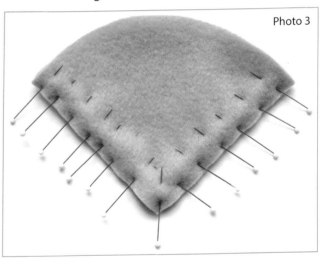

Photo 3

When preparing to sew through several layers of fabric, decrease the presser foot pressure or try pushing up on the presser foot bar raising it just a bit to accommodate the greater thickness. Insert fabric layers under the presser foot and then lower it.

It is also sometimes helpful to have fabric scraps to use as starters. Fold scraps to make them as thick as the pieces being sewn. Place folded scrap behind puzzle ball pieces and under the back of the presser foot.

To get started when sewing through thick layers, wrap the upper and lower thread ends around the index finger of your left hand (Photo 4) and give them a tug as you make the first few stitches. This will get the sewing started without creating a nest of bobbin thread.

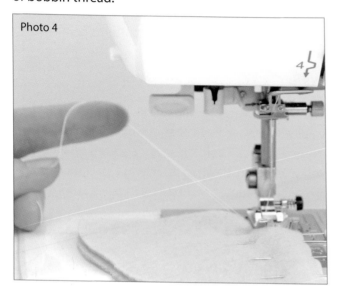

Photo 4

The standard recommended stitch length is 2.5mm or about 10–12 stitches per inch. A stitch length of 2.2mm is recommended for these projects. The smaller the stitch length number, the shorter the stitch length. Using short stitches will help increase accuracy and ensure a tight seam that can be stuffed firmly.

Backstitch at the start and end of each seam, especially on either side of the openings, to be sure the stitches don't come undone.

Sew with all-purpose polyester thread in a color that matches your fabric. It's strong and less apt to break under the stress of stuffing and playing with the puzzle balls. You can use a buttonhole twist or topstitching thread to hand-stitch the pieces of the puzzle ball together to create the body units.

There is no need to press the seams open for these projects. If you do need to press the fleece for any reason, use a warm iron, not a hot iron, to avoid melting the fabric.

Making a Standard Puzzle Ball Segment

Each puzzle ball is made up of three rings and each ring is made up of four segments (Photo 5).

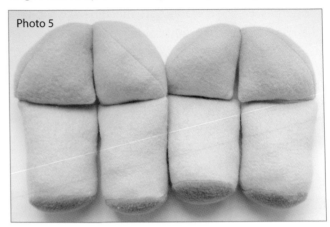

Photo 5

1. Prepare wedge and cap patterns from pattern paper.

2. Position and pin two wedges right sides together. Leave top curved edge and seam between squares open (Photo 6).

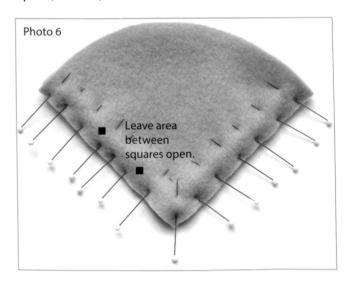

Photo 6

Leave area between squares open.

3. Open wedge curved edge and pin to either side of cap matching circles on wedge and cap; stitch (Photo 7).

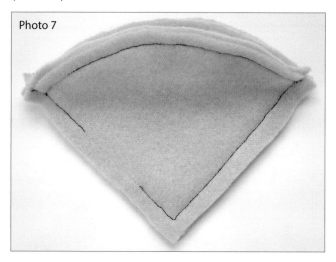
Photo 7

4. Clip curves and trim corners to reduce bulk (Photo 8). Turn segment right sides out through side opening.

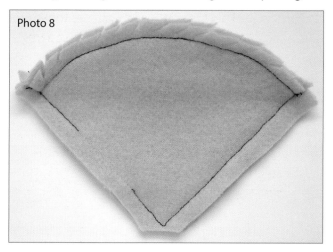
Photo 8

5. Stuff firmly referring to Stuffing Segments. Close the opening with a ladder stitch.

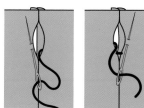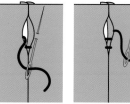

Ladder Stitch

6. Prepare leg and foot pad patterns. Cut eight legs and four foot pads.

Stuffing Segments

Each segment of the puzzle ball should be firmly stuffed. You can use your fingers, a chopstick or a pair of hemostats to insert the fiberfill.

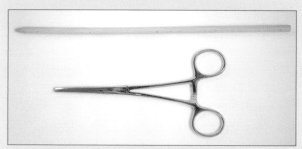

Go slowly, using small wads of polyester fiberfill at a time and taking care that there are no lumps or hollow spots. Push small bits of fiberfill into the corners or extremities of each piece.

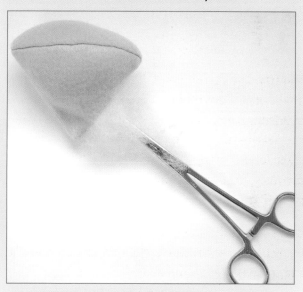

The fiberfill will compress over time, so it's best to use more than you think is necessary, especially on the heads and legs of the puzzle balls. After stuffing as full as desired, roll the piece gently in your hands to compact the fiberfill and even out its placement.

Close the opening using a ladder stitch referring to Joining Sides With a Ladder Stitch on page 8.

Joining Sides With a Ladder Stitch

Use a ladder stitch to create an invisible closure after you've stuffed the segment, or to attach specific parts to your puzzle balls.

Thread a needle with a double length of all-purpose thread and tie a knot at the end. Bring the needle into the opening, coming up through the seam close to where the opening begins. Place a small stitch parallel with the opening on one side, then on the other.

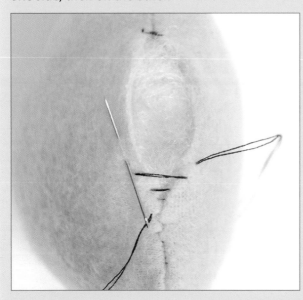

Continue stitching, pulling the thread tight every few stitches. At the end of the opening take a small stitch, passing the needle through the loop to create a wrap knot.

Insert the needle at the knot and bring it out a few inches away. Pull the thread tight, then cut it so that the thread end gets pulled back into the stuffed segment.

A ladder stitch can also be used to attach specific parts, such as the giraffe's ears and the bumblebee's nose. For these it's best to stitch around the piece twice to ensure a secure attachment.

7. Stitch two legs right sides together, leaving open at side between squares, and at bottom edge.

8. Position and pin a foot pad over the open end of the assembled leg, right sides together, aligning two foot pad triangles with the leg seams and remaining triangles (Photo 9). Use several more pins to pin the foot pad to the leg.

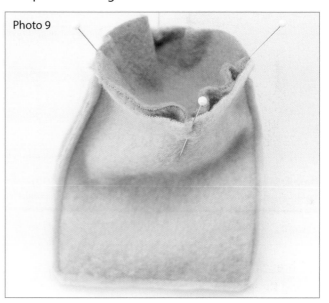

Photo 9

9. Machine-stitch foot pad to leg (Photo 10). Clip curves and turn leg right side out through side opening. Stuff firmly and close the opening with ladder stitch.

Photo 10

10. Repeat steps 7–9 to make four leg segments.

Forming Puzzle Ball Rings

1. To assemble a ring, place four segments on your worktable with the tips of the wedges pointed toward the center (Photo 11). Begin by attaching two segments to one another at the top corner.

Photo 11

2. Thread a needle with a double length of extra-strong thread, like buttonhole twist thread. Insert the needle through the seam at the side of segment, coming out at the corner (Photo 12).

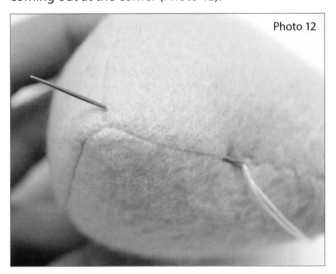

Photo 12

3. Pull on the thread until the knot pops through the stitches of the seam. Stitch through the corner of the next segment, then back through the first segment, pulling on the thread to pull the two segments close to one another. Repeat at least three more times to create a secure attachment (Photo 13).

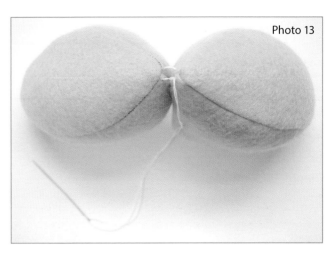

Photo 13

4. Pass the thread through the stitches, then through the thread loop to create a wrap knot.

5. Insert the needle at the knot and bring it out a few inches away. Pull the thread tight, then cut it so that the thread end is pulled back into the stuffed segment (Photo 14). Stitch together remaining segments to complete the ring.

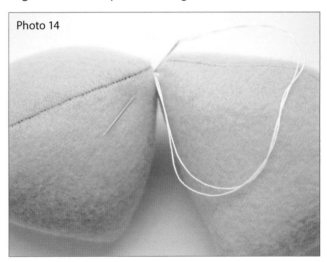

Photo 14

Giving Your Puzzle Balls Faces

Your puzzle balls won't be complete without their expressive and friendly faces. You can embroider all the details of the faces or choose to mix embroidered details with safety eyes.

Properly inserted safety eyes are very secure, but can still pose a safety hazard for children under age three. When making a puzzle ball for a very young child, embroider the eyes with satin stitch.

Inserting Safety Eyes

The patterns in this book call for 8mm black safety eyes. Be careful when inserting safety eyes; once you poke a hole in your fabric and insert the eye, it cannot be removed.

1. To insert a safety eye, make a small hole with the tip of a pair of embroidery scissors or a ballpoint awl (Photo 15).

Photo 15

2. Push the safety eye post through the hole from the front of the fabric to the back.

3. Slide the safety eye washer, rounded side up, onto the post, pushing it all the way down until the eye and the washer are flush with the fabric and you hear a pop.

4. Stuff your puzzle ball head.

Embroidering a Face

1. Embroider the face after stuffing to determine the best placement. Mark the face with a removable fabric marker.

2. Thread an embroidery needle with either three strands of 6-ply embroidery floss or No. 8 pearl cotton and tie a small, tight knot in the end.

3. Insert the needle through a seam in the face, coming up where you want to begin embroidering (Photo 16). Pull the floss until the knot pops through the stitches in the seam.

Photo 16

4. Use a satin stitch or backstitch to embroider the face. You may also use a French knot to create the lion's whiskers.

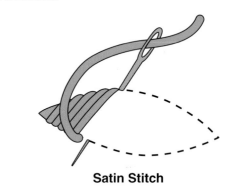

Satin Stitch

Backstitch

French Knot

5. Place a small stitch at the end of the embroidery to secure. Bringing the needle out a few inches away, pull the floss tight, and then cut it so that the thread end is pulled back into the stuffed segment.

Assembling the Puzzle Ball

Each puzzle ball is made up of three rings. For most of them, rings 1 and 2 are made up of two legs and two standard segments. Ring 3 is made up of two standard segments plus a head and a tail segment (Photo 17).

Photo 17

Putting the puzzle ball together is, well, puzzling … unless you know the secret.

Begin by interlocking the two rings that have legs. Slip one leg through the center of the other ring (Photo 18).

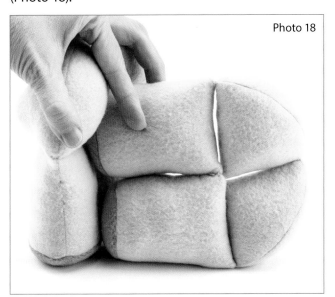

Photo 18

Straighten the legs out and be sure the pointy tips of the segments are pointing toward the center (Photo 19). The legs will now stand up on their own.

Photo 19

Slide the ring with the head and tail over the top of the leg rings and down, centered on the leg segments (Photo 20). ●

Photo 20

Need assembly help?
Video Tutorial
AVAILABLE AT
ANNIESCRAFTSTORE.COM

Elephant

This delightful elephant is fun to cuddle and to play with. You can sew him up using a traditional gray fabric, but light blue is also very sweet.

Skill Level
Confident Beginner

Finished Size
Puzzle Ball Size: 7 x 7 x 10 inches

Materials
- ¼ yard dark blue fleece
- ½ yard light blue fleece
- 2 (8mm) black safety eyes with washers
- 18 inches black embroidery floss or No. 8 pearl cotton
- 6 ounces polyester fiberfill
- Thread
- Basic sewing supplies and equipment

Project Notes
Read all instructions before beginning this project.

Stitch right sides together using a ¼-inch seam allowance unless otherwise specified.

Materials and cutting lists assume 54 inches of usable fabric width.

All pattern pieces are included on pages 41, 47 and 48.

Cutting
Transfer all markings from the pattern pieces after cutting.

From dark blue fleece:
- Cut: 4 Foot Pads
  - 2 Elephant Ears (reverse 1)
  - 2 Elephant Tail Tips

From light blue fleece:
- Cut: 16 Wedges
  - 7 Caps
  - 8 Legs
  - 2 Elephant Ears (reverse 1)
  - 2 Elephant Faces (reverse 1)
  - 2 Elephant Tails

Completing Rings 1 & 2
Rings 1 and 2 each consist of two standard segments and two leg segments.

1. For each ring, follow instructions for Making a Standard Puzzle Ball Segment on page 6 to create two standard segments from light blue fleece and two light blue fleece legs with dark blue feet.

2. Position two legs side by side, with two standard segments above and triangular tips pointing inward (Photo 1). Using buttonhole twist thread and, following instructions for Forming Puzzle Ball Rings on page 9, stitch the ring together.

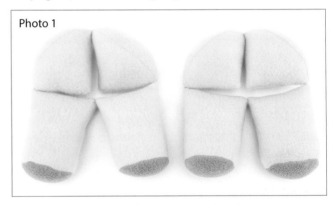

Photo 1

3. Repeat steps 1 and 2 to create ring 2.

Completing Ring 3

Ring 3 consists of two standard segments, a head and a tail.

1. Following instructions for Making a Standard Puzzle Ball Segment on page 6, create two standard segments from light blue fleece.

2. Prepare tail, tail tip, ear and face patterns from pattern paper.

3. To create tail, layer one each tail and tail tip piece right sides together, and stitch together between small circles. Repeat with the other tail tip and tail piece.

4. Position and pin assembled tail pieces right sides together, matching seams. Stitch leaving straight edge along bottom open. Clip curves and trim seam allowance on tip of tail to reduce bulk. Turn right side out.

5. Stuff tip of the tail firmly, leaving remainder unstuffed.

6. Center assembled tail on right side of cap aligning raw edges with the edge of cap. Baste in place. Sew segment following instructions for Making a Standard Puzzle Ball Segment on page 6, catching raw edges of the tail in the seam between the cap and one wedge. Remove basting stitches. Turn segment right side out, stuff firmly and close opening with ladder stitch found on pages 7 and 8 (Photo 2).

Photo 2

7. Pin and stitch a light blue ear right sides together with a dark blue ear, leaving open between squares. Clip curves and turn right side out. Repeat to create a second ear.

8. Position ears with dark blue side up and fold the top of each ear along fold line (Photo 3); baste.

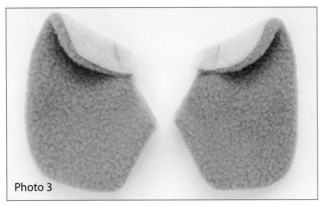

Photo 3

9. Position and pin two elephant faces right sides together (Photo 4A). Sew from small circle around trunk to large circle. Stitch darts closed on head (Photo 4B).

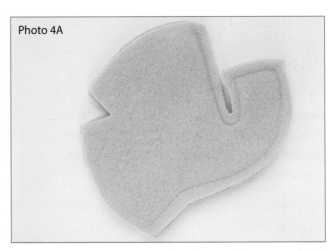

Photo 4A

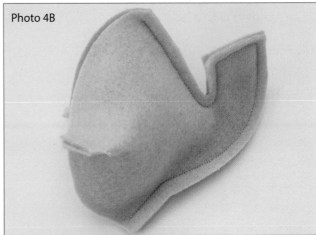

Photo 4B

10. Baste ears between squares on assembled head with dark blue side against head (Photo 5).

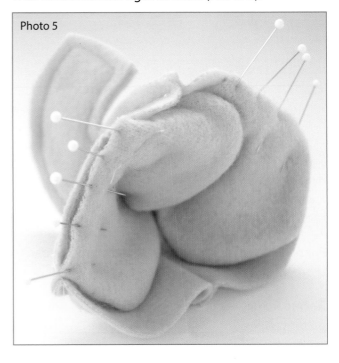

Photo 5

11. Position and pin two wedges right sides together. Sew sides, leaving top curved edge and side opening unstitched.

12. Position and pin assembled head on assembled wedge, right sides together, aligning wedge seams with darts on each side of head. Stitch, clip seam allowance and remove basting stitches. Turn segment right side out.

13. Following instructions for Inserting Safety Eyes on page 10, attach safety eyes to face as marked. Stuff firmly referring to Stuffing Segments on page 7. Close opening with a ladder stitch.

14. Following instructions for Embroidering a Face, embroider mouth with a backstitch as shown on page 10.

15. Position a standard segment, the head, a standard segment and the tail clockwise in a circle (Photo 6). ***Note:*** *The tail is on the upper portion of the segment.* Using buttonhole twist thread and following the instructions for Forming Puzzle Ball Rings on page 9, stitch the four segments of the ring together.

Photo 6

16. Interlock the three rings referring to Assembling the Puzzle Ball on page 11 to create your elephant puzzle ball. ●

Dinosaur

Don't be frightened by our prehistoric friend! This dinosaur might look fierce, but he's really cuddly and lots of fun. Dinosaurs are always popular with toddlers and with young children, and this one will make a great gift!

Skill Level
Confident Beginner

Finished Size
Puzzle Ball Size: 8 x 10 x 15 inches

Materials
- ¼ yard bright green fleece
- ½ yard dark green mottled fleece
- 2 (8mm) black safety eyes with washers
- 18 inches black embroidery floss or No. 8 pearl cotton
- 8½ ounces polyester fiberfill
- Thread
- Basic sewing supplies and equipment

Project Notes
Read all instructions before beginning this project.

Stitch right sides together using a ¼-inch seam allowance unless otherwise specified.

Materials and cutting lists assume 54 inches of usable fabric width.

All pattern pieces are included on pages 41–43.

Cutting
Transfer all markings from the pattern pieces after cutting.

From bright green fleece:
- Cut: 4 Foot Pads
  2 Dinosaur Back Spikes
  2 Dinosaur Head Spikes

From dark green mottled fleece:
- Cut: 16 Wedges
  6 Caps
  8 Legs
  2 Dinosaur Faces (reverse 1)
  2 Dinosaur Tails (reverse 1)

Completing Rings 1 and 2
Rings 1 and 2 consist of two standard segments and two leg segments each.

1. For each ring, follow instructions for Making a Standard Puzzle Ball Segment on page 6 to create two standard segments from dark green fleece and two legs from dark green fleece with bright green feet.

2. Position two legs side by side, with two standard segments above, triangular tips pointing inward (Photo 1). Using buttonhole twist thread and following instructions for Forming Puzzle Ball Rings on page 9, stitch the ring together.

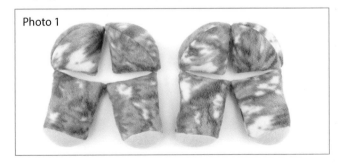

Photo 1

3. Repeat steps 1 and 2 to create ring 2.

Completing Ring 3

Ring 3 consists of two standard segments, a head and a tail.

1. Following instructions for Making a Standard Puzzle Ball Segment on page 6, create two standard segments from dark green fleece.

2. Prepare back and head spikes, and head patterns from pattern paper.

3. Position and pin back spikes right sides together. Stitch leaving the long straight edge at the bottom open (Photo 2). Clip seams, especially between each triangle, and trim seam allowance at the tip of each spike. Turn right side out and carefully push out each spike.

Photo 2

4. Stitch darts closed on the two tail pieces (Photo 3).

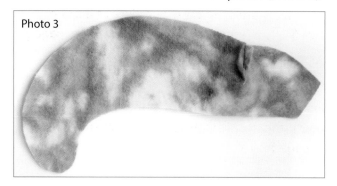
Photo 3

5. Position and pin spikes on one tail piece, right sides together opposite from dart, matching small and large circles; baste (Photo 4).

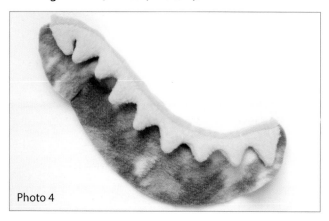
Photo 4

6. Position and pin the second tail piece on top, right sides together. Stitch from small circle to large circle catching spikes in seam, and then stitch from large circle to square referring to Photo 5.

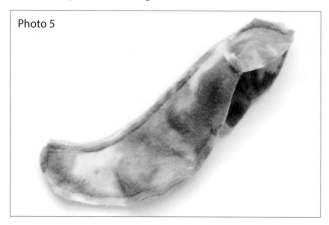
Photo 5

7. Position and pin two wedges right sides together. Sew sides, leaving top curved edge and side opening unstitched. Position and pin assembled tail on assembled wedge, right sides together, aligning wedge seams with darts on each side of tail (Photo 6). Stitch, clip seam allowance and remove basting stitches. Turn segment right side out.

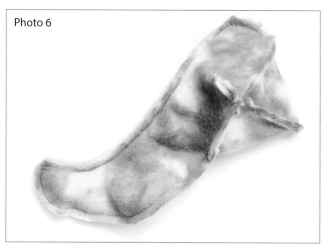
Photo 6

8. Stuff firmly referring to Stuffing Segments on page 7. Close opening with a ladder stitch found on pages 7 and 8.

9. Position and pin two head spikes right sides together. Stitch leaving the long straight edge at the bottom open (Photo 7). Clip seams, especially between each triangle, and trim seam allowance at the tip of each spike. Turn right side out and carefully push out each spike.

Photo 7

10. Stitch darts closed on both head pieces.

11. Position and pin spikes on one head piece, right sides together, between squares (Photo 8); baste.

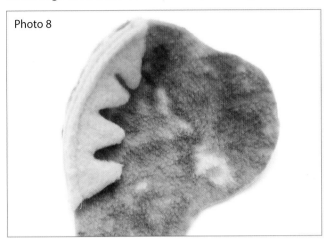
Photo 8

12. Position and pin the second head piece on top, right sides together. Stitch from square at bottom of spikes around the head and down the neck front to large square.

13. Position and pin two wedges right sides together. Sew sides, leaving top curved edge and side opening unstitched.

14. Position and pin assembled head to assembled wedge, right sides together, matching wedge seams to darts on each side of neck; stitch (Photo 9). Clip seam allowance and remove basting stitches. Turn segment right side out.

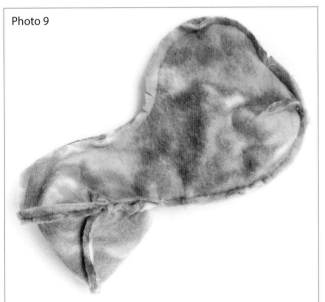
Photo 9

15. Following instructions for Inserting Safety Eyes on page 10, attach safety eyes to face as marked. Stuff firmly referring to Stuffing Segments on page 7. Close opening with a ladder stitch.

16. Following instructions for Embroidering a Face and referring to photo for placement, embroider mouth and nostrils with a backstitch as shown on page 10.

17. Position a standard segment, the head, a standard segment and the tail clockwise in a circle (Photo 10). Using buttonhole twist thread and following the instructions for Forming Puzzle Ball Rings on page 9, stitch the four segments of the ring together.

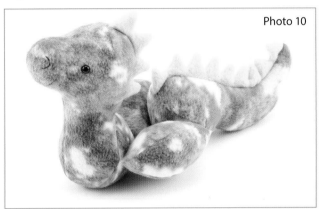
Photo 10

18. Interlock the three rings referring to Assembling the Puzzle Ball on page 11 to create your dinosaur puzzle ball. ●

Giraffe

Giraffes are elegant creatures, and they're lovable as stuffed animals too. Giraffe print fleece makes this giraffe puzzle ball adorable, but if you can't find it, you can use yellow fleece instead. Either way, it's sure to be a hit!

Skill Level
Confident Beginner

Finished Size
Puzzle Ball Size: 7 x 9 x 12 inches

Materials
- ¼ yard peach fleece
- ½ yard giraffe print fleece
- 2 (8mm) black safety eyes with washers
- 18 inches black embroidery floss or No. 8 pearl cotton
- 8½ ounces polyester fiberfill
- Thread
- Basic sewing supplies and equipment

Project Notes
Read all instructions before beginning this project.

Stitch right sides together using a ¼-inch seam allowance unless otherwise specified.

Materials and cutting lists assume 54 inches of usable fabric width.

All pattern pieces are included on pages 41, 44 and 47.

Cutting
Transfer all markings from the pattern pieces after cutting.

From peach fleece:
- Cut: 4 Foot Pads
     2 Giraffe Ears
     2 Giraffe Tail Tips
     4 Giraffe Horns
     2 Giraffe Muzzles (reverse 1)
- Cut 1 (1 x 3¼-inch) strip for mane.

From giraffe print fleece:
- Cut: 16 Wedges
     7 Caps
     8 Legs
     2 Giraffe Ears
     2 Giraffe Tails
     2 Giraffe Heads (reverse 1)

Completing Rings 1 and 2
Rings 1 and 2 consist of two standard segments and two leg segments each.

1. For each ring, follow instructions for Making a Standard Puzzle Ball Segment on page 6 to create two standard segments from giraffe print fleece and two legs from giraffe print fleece with peach feet.

2. Position two legs side by side, with two standard segments above, triangular tips pointing inward (Photo 1). Using buttonhole twist thread and following instructions for Forming Puzzle Ball Rings on page 9, stitch the ring together.

Photo 1

3. Repeat steps 1 and 2 to create ring 2.

Completing Ring 3
Ring 3 consists of two standard segments, a head and a tail.

1. Following instructions for Making a Standard Puzzle Ball Segment on page 6, create two standard segments from giraffe print fleece.

2. Prepare tail, tail tip, ear, face, horn and muzzle patterns from pattern paper.

3. To create tail, layer one each tail and tail tip piece right sides together, and stitch together between small circles. Repeat with the other tail tip and tail piece.

4. Position and pin assembled tail pieces right sides together, matching seams. Stitch leaving straight edge along bottom open. Clip curves and trim seam allowance on tip of tail to reduce bulk. Turn right side out.

5. Stuff tip of the tail firmly, leaving remainder unstuffed.

6. Center assembled tail on right side of cap aligning raw edges with the edge of cap. Baste in place. Sew segment following instructions for Making a Standard Puzzle Ball Segment on page 6, catching raw edges of the tail in the seam between the cap and one wedge. Remove basting stitches. Turn segment right side out, stuff firmly and close opening with ladder stitch found on pages 7 and 8.

7. Position and pin one muzzle piece on one face piece, right sides together, aligning circles (Photo 2). Repeat for the other muzzle and face piece.

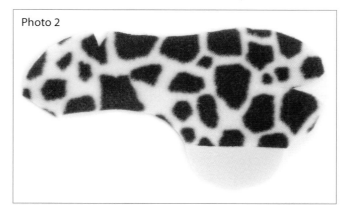
Photo 2

8. Position and pin horns right sides together. Stitch leaving straight edge at bottom open. Clip curves and turn right side out. Stuff firmly, leaving ¼ inch at the bottom unstuffed. Repeat to create a second horn.

9. Position horn on the right side of face aligning raw edges of the horn with the curve of the dart at the top of the head (Photo 3).

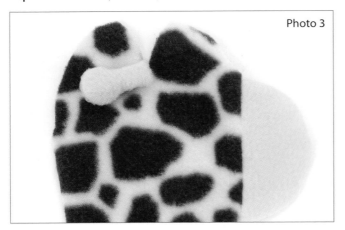

Photo 3

10. Stitch face dart closed, catching the raw edges of the horn in the seam (Photo 4). Repeat to attach the other horn to the left side of face.

Photo 4

11. Fold the mane strip in half, wrong sides together. Position it on one face piece, right sides together, between squares; baste (Photo 5). **Note:** *The mane will be clipped after the face is sewn and turned.*

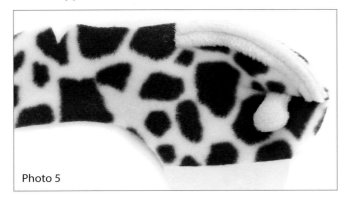

Photo 5

12. Stitch the lower dart on each face piece. Position and pin the two face pieces right sides together. Stitch from the square at base of mane around the head and down the neck front to large square, catching the raw edges of the mane in the seam.

13. Position and pin two wedges right sides together. Sew sides, leaving top curved edge and side opening unstitched.

14. Position and pin assembled head to assembled wedge, right sides together, matching wedge seams to darts on each side of head; stitch. Clip seam allowance and remove basting stitches. Turn segment right side out.

15. Following instructions for Inserting Safety Eyes on page 10, attach safety eyes to face as marked. Stuff firmly referring to Stuffing Segments on page 7. Close opening with a ladder stitch. Make short clips every ¼ inch in the mane.

16. Pin a peach ear right sides together with a giraffe print ear. Stitch leaving open along straight bottom edge. Clip curves and turn right side out. Repeat to create a second ear.

17. Position ears peach side up and fold each ear along fold line (Photo 6); baste.

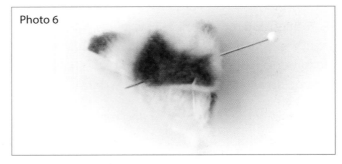

Photo 6

18. Fold raw edges of the ears under ⅛ inch and baste. Pin ears to the giraffe's head as marked. Ladder-stitch ears to head, going around twice for added strength.

19. Following instructions for Embroidering a Face, embroider mouth and nostrils with a backstitch as shown on page 10 (Photo 7).

Photo 7

20. Position a standard segment, the head, a standard segment and the tail clockwise in a circle (Photo 8). ***Note:*** *The tail is on the upper portion of the segment.* Using buttonhole twist thread and following the instructions for Forming Puzzle Ball Rings on page 9, stitch the four segments of the ring together.

Photo 8

21. Interlock the three rings referring to Assembling the Puzzle Ball on page 11 to create your giraffe puzzle ball. ●

Bunny

Hippety-hop! Sew this bunny in soft white and pink fleece to make a perfect springtime gift. Bunny's bouncy pompom tail is the perfect finishing touch.

Skill Level
Confident Beginner

Finished Size
Puzzle Ball Size: 7" x 7" x 8"

Materials
- ¼ yard light pink fleece
- ½ yard white fleece
- 2 (8mm) black safety eyes with washers
- 18 inches each brown and black embroidery floss or No. 8 pearl cotton
- 6 ounces polyester fiberfill
- Thread
- Lipstick to blush cheeks (optional)
- Basic sewing supplies and equipment

Project Notes
Read all instructions before beginning this project.

Stitch right sides together using a ¼-inch seam allowance unless otherwise specified.

Materials and cutting lists assume 54 inches of usable fabric width.

All patterns are included on pages 41 and 45.

Cutting
Transfer all markings from the pattern pieces after cutting.

From light pink fleece:
- Cut: 2 Bunny Ears
      4 Foot Pads

From white fleece:
- Cut: 16 Wedges
      7 Caps
      8 Legs
      2 Bunny Ears
      1 Bunny Face
- Cut 1 (15 x 2-inch) strip for pompom.
- Cut 1 (⅛ x 8-inch) strip. Cut parallel to the grain for tail tie.

Completing Rings 1 and 2
Rings 1 and 2 each consist of two standard segments and two leg segments.

1. For each ring, follow instructions for Making a Standard Puzzle Ball Segment on page 6 to create two standard segments from white fleece and two legs from white fleece with light pink feet.

2. Position two legs side by side, with two standard segments above, triangular tips pointing inward, to form a ring of segments (Photo 1). Using buttonhole twist thread and following instructions for Forming Puzzle Ball Rings on page 9, stitch the ring together.

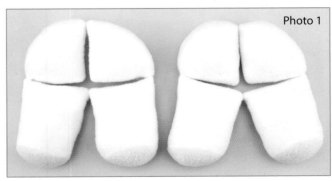

Photo 1

3. Repeat steps 1 and 2 to create ring 2.

Completing Ring 3

Ring 3 consists of two standard segments, a head and a tail.

1. Following instructions for Making a Standard Puzzle Ball Segment on page 6, create two standard segments from white fleece.

2. Prepare ear and face patterns from pattern paper.

3. Make ¾-inch-long snips at ¼-inch intervals along one side of the 2 x 15-inch fleece strip. Repeat

snipping along the other side, preserving an uncut area down the center of the strip (Photo 2).

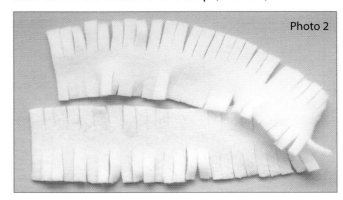

Photo 2

4. Tightly roll the strip. Using the ⅛ x 8-inch strip of fleece, tie a double knot around the center to make a pompom. Leaving the two long tails of the tie, trim the pompom to make a round, fluffy ball (Photo 3).

Photo 3

5. Center assembled pompom on right side of cap very close to the edge, with the long ends of the tie extending off the edge of the cap; baste. Sew segment following instructions for Making a Standard Puzzle Ball Segment on page 6, catching raw edges of the tie in the seam between the cap and one wedge. Remove basting stitches. Turn segment right side out, stuff firmly and close opening with ladder stitch found on pages 7 and 8 (Photo 4).

Photo 4

6. Pin and stitch a light pink ear right sides together with a white ear, leaving the straight bottom edge open. Clip curves and turn right side out. Fold in half along fold line and pin (Photo 5). Repeat to create a second ear.

Photo 5

7. Stitch the four darts on the face closed (Photo 6).

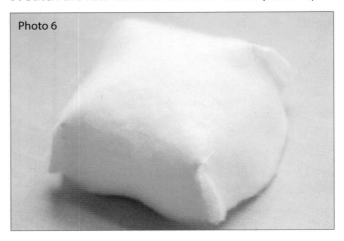

Photo 6

8. Position and pin ears on the right side of the face between the large squares making sure the light pink portions are facing each another (Photo 7). Baste.

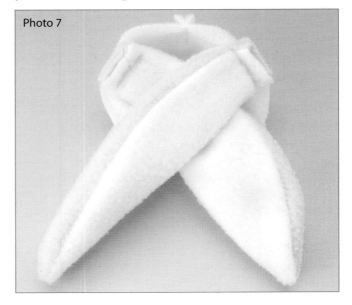

Photo 7

9. Position and pin two wedges right sides together. Sew sides, leaving top curved edge and side opening unstitched. Position and pin assembled head on assembled wedge, right sides together, matching wedge seams to darts on each side of head. Stitch, clip seam allowance and remove basting stitches. Turn segment right side out.

10. Following instructions for Inserting Safety Eyes on page 10, attach safety eyes to face as marked. Stuff firmly referring to Stuffing Segments on page 7. Close opening with a ladder stitch.

11. Following instructions for Embroidering a Face on page 10, embroider the nose with satin stitch and the mouth with backstitch. If desired, blush the cheeks with a light application of lipstick. Take two straight stitches with black embroidery floss on either side of the eyes to create eyelashes.

12. Work clockwise when positioning the remaining four segments. Place a standard segment, the head, a standard segment and the tail segment (with the tail up) in a circle (Photo 8). Using buttonhole twist thread and following the instructions for Forming Puzzle Ball Rings on page 9, stitch the four segments of the ring together.

Photo 8

13. Interlock the three rings referring to Assembling the Puzzle Ball on page 11 to create your bunny puzzle ball. ●

Bumblebee

Buzz, buzz! This bumblebee puzzle ball is sweet as honey.
And don't worry—he promises not to sting!

Skill Level
Confident Beginner

Finished Size
Puzzle Ball Size: 7 x 7 x 7 inches

Materials
- ¼ yard white fleece
- ½ yard yellow fleece
- ½ yard black fleece
- 2 (8mm) black safety eyes with washers
- 18 inches black embroidery floss or No. 8 pearl cotton
- 6 ounces polyester fiberfill
- Thread
- Basic sewing supplies and equipment

Project Notes
Read all instructions before beginning this project.

Stitch right sides together using a ¼-inch seam allowance unless otherwise specified.

Materials and cutting lists assume 54 inches of usable fabric width.

All patterns are included on pages 41 and 46.

Cutting
Transfer all markings from the pattern pieces after cutting.

From white fleece:
- Cut 4 each Bumblebee Large Wings and Small Wings.

From yellow fleece:
- Cut: 11 Caps
       1 Bumblebee Nose
       1 Bumblebee Face

From black fleece:
- Cut: 24 Wedges
       2 Bumblebee Stingers
       4 Bumblebee Antennae (reverse 2)

Completing Rings 1 and 2
Rings 1 and 2 each consist of four standard segments.

1. For each ring, follow instructions for Making a Standard Puzzle Ball Segment on page 6 to create eight standard segments from black wedges and yellow caps for each ring.

2. Position four standard segments, triangular tips pointing inward, to form a ring of segments. Using buttonhole twist thread and following instructions for Forming Puzzle Ball Rings on page 9, stitch the ring together.

Photo 1

3. Repeat steps 1 and 2 to create ring 2.

Completing Ring 3

Ring 3 consists of two wing segments, a face segment and a stinger segment.

1. Prepare large and small wings, stingers, antennae and nose patterns from pattern paper.

2. Position and pin two large wings right sides together. Stitch leaving the straight edge at the bottom open. Clip curves and turn right side out. Topstitch ¼ inch from edge. Repeat to make a second large wing.

3. Repeat step 2 to make two small wings.

4. Position and pin two wedges right sides together. Sew sides, leaving top curved edge and side opening unstitched. Position and pin one each large and small wing, right sides together, on assembled wedge aligning raw edges. Roll the wings up so they fit inside the segment and baste (Photo 2). Repeat to create a second segment that is a mirror image of the first.

Photo 2

5. Sew segment following instructions for Making a Standard Puzzle Ball Segment on page 6. Remove basting stitches. Turn segment right side out, stuff firmly and close opening with ladder stitch found on pages 7 and 8.

6. Position and pin stingers right sides together. Stitch leaving straight edge along bottom open. Clip curves and trim seam allowance on tip to reduce bulk. Turn right side out.

7. Position and pin two wedges right sides together. Sew sides, leaving top curved edge and side opening unstitched. Position and pin stinger on assembled wedge, right sides together. Baste.

8. Sew segment following instructions for Making a Standard Puzzle Ball Segment on page 6, catching raw edges of stinger in the seam between the cap and one wedge. Remove basting stitches. Turn segment right side out, stuff firmly and close opening with ladder stitch (Photo 3).

Photo 3

9. Position and pin two antennae right sides together. Stitch leaving straight edge along bottom open. Clip curves and turn right side out. Push a small amount of fiberfill inside the circular part of the antenna, stuffing it firmly and leaving the remainder unstuffed. Repeat to make two (Photo 4).

Photo 4

10. Stitch the four darts on the face closed (Photo 5).

Photo 5

11. Pinch antennae so the seam runs down the center. Place antennae on the right side of face at small circles making sure the antennae are curved downward (Photo 6). Baste.

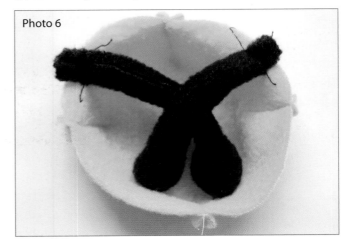
Photo 6

12. Position and pin two wedges right sides together. Sew sides, leaving top curved edge and side opening unstitched. Position and pin assembled head on assembled wedge, right sides together, aligning wedge seams with darts on each side of head. Stitch, clip seam allowance and remove basting stitches. Turn segment right side out.

13. Following instructions for Inserting Safety Eyes on page 10, attach safety eyes to face as marked. Stuff firmly referring to Stuffing Segments on page 7. Close opening with a ladder stitch.

14. Use a running stitch and sew ⅛ inch inside the nose, going all the way around. Pull the stitches to gather the nose (Photo 7).

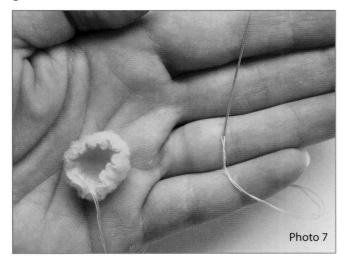

Photo 7

15. Push a small bit of fiberfill inside the nose, and then pull the stitches tight and tie off in a double knot. Pin the nose to the face and ladder-stitch in place, going around twice to be sure it is securely attached (Photo 8).

Photo 8

16. Following instructions for Embroidering a Face, embroider mouth with a backstitch as shown on page 10.

17. Work clockwise when positioning the remaining four segments. Place a wing segment (wing side up), the head, a wing segment and the tail segment (tail side up) in a circle (Photo 9).

Photo 9

Using buttonhole twist thread and following the instructions for Forming Puzzle Ball Rings on page 9, stitch the four segments of the ring together.

18. Interlock the three rings referring to Assembling the Puzzle Ball on page 11 to create your bumblebee puzzle ball. ●

Lion

This lion puzzle ball is a little ferocious and a lot of fun. Choose warm, bright colors, especially for the mane. This is the king of the jungle after all!

Skill Level
Confident Beginner

Finished Size
Puzzle Ball Size: 7 x 7 x 7 inches

Materials
- Scraps white and red fleece
- ½ yard yellow print fleece
- 2 (8mm) black safety eyes with washers
- 18 inches brown embroidery floss or No. 8 pearl cotton
- 6 ounces polyester fiberfill
- Thread
- Basic sewing supplies and equipment

Project Notes
Read all instructions before beginning this project.

Stitch right sides together using a ¼-inch seam allowance unless otherwise specified.

Materials and cutting lists assume 54 inches of usable fabric width.

All patterns are included on pages 41 and 47.

Cutting
Transfer all markings from the pattern pieces after cutting.

From white fleece:
- Cut 1 Lion Muzzle and 2 Lion Tail Tips.

From red fleece:
- Cut 2 Lion Manes and 4 Foot Pads.

From yellow print fleece:
- Cut: 16 Wedges
   - 7 Caps
   - 8 Legs
   - 4 Lion Ears
   - 1 Lion Head
   - 2 Lion Tails

Completing Rings 1 and 2
Rings 1 and 2 each consist of two standard segments and two leg segments.

1. For each ring, follow instructions for Making a Standard Puzzle Ball Segment on page 6 to create two standard segments and two legs with red feet from yellow print fleece.

2. Position two legs side by side, with two standard segments above, triangular tips pointing inward, to form a ring of segments (Photo 1). Using buttonhole twist thread and following instructions for Forming Puzzle Ball Rings on page 9, stitch the ring together.

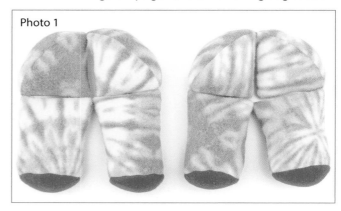
Photo 1

3. Repeat steps 1 and 2 to create ring 2.

Completing Ring 3
Ring 3 consists of two standard segments, a head and a tail.

1. Following instructions for Making a Standard Puzzle Ball Segment on page 6, create two standard segments from yellow print fleece.

2. Prepare tail, tail tip, ear, head, muzzle and mane patterns from pattern paper.

3. To create tail, layer tail tip and tail, right sides together, and stitch between small circles. Repeat with the other tail tip and tail piece.

4. Position and pin assembled tail pieces right sides together, matching seams. Stitch leaving straight edge along bottom open (Photo 2). Clip curves and trim seam allowance on tip of tail to reduce bulk. Turn right side out.

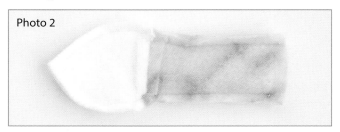
Photo 2

5. Stuff tip of the tail firmly, leaving remainder unstuffed.

6. Center assembled tail on right side of cap aligning raw edges with the edge of cap. Baste in place (Photo 3).

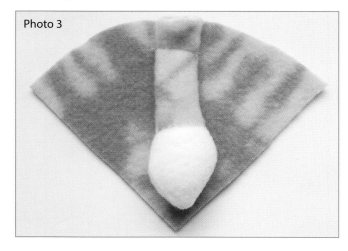
Photo 3

7. Sew segment following instructions for Making a Standard Puzzle Ball Segment on page 6, catching raw edges of the tail in the seam between the cap and one wedge. Remove basting stitches. Turn segment right side out, stuff firmly and close opening with ladder stitch found on pages 7 and 8 (Photo 4).

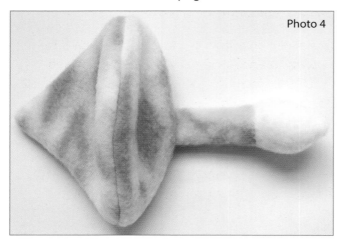

Photo 4

8. Pin two ears right sides together and stitch leaving opening along straight bottom. Clip curves and turn right side out. Repeat to create a second ear.

9. Position and pin two mane pieces right sides together. Stitch outer curved edge, between circles, leaving the inner circular edge open (Photo 5). Clip curves and turn right side out, being sure to poke out the curved parts of the mane.

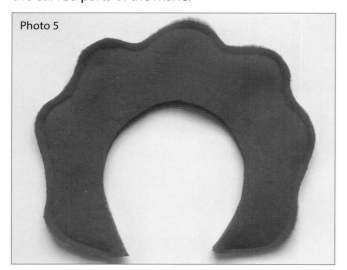

Photo 5

10. Position and pin the muzzle on the head, right sides together, aligning triangle (Photo 6).

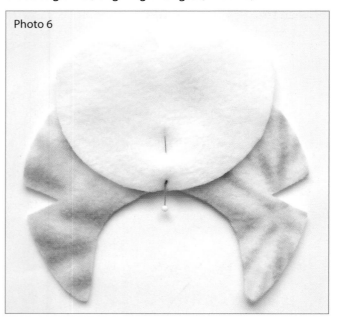

Photo 6

11. Align remaining points on the head and muzzle and pin (Photo 7). Stitch from left-hand circle through triangle to right-hand circle.

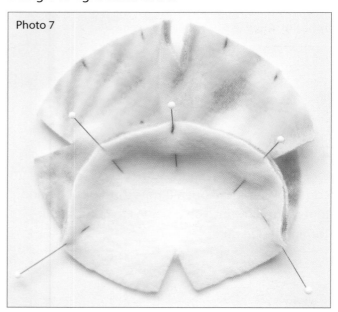

Photo 7

12. Stitch darts on face as marked.

13. Position and pin ears on the face, aligning the raw edges of the ears with the edge of the face between squares (Photo 8). Baste.

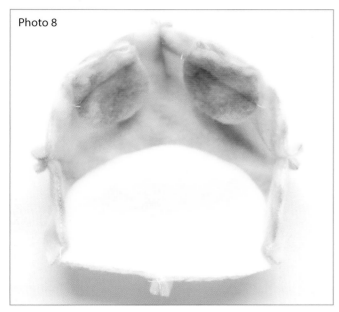

Photo 8

14. Position and pin mane on the head, matching square on mane with the center dart seam on the head. Align circles on mane with circles on muzzle (Photo 9). Baste.

Photo 9

15. Position and pin two wedges right sides together. Sew sides, leaving top curved edge and side opening unstitched. Position and pin assembled head on assembled wedge, right sides together, aligning wedge seams with darts on each side of head. Stitch, clip seam allowance and remove basting stitches. Turn segment right side out.

16. Following instructions for Inserting Safety Eyes on page 10, attach safety eyes to face as marked. Stuff firmly referring to Stuffing Segments on page 7. Close opening with a ladder stitch.

17. Following instructions for Embroidering a Face on page 10, embroider the nose with a satin stitch, the mouth with a backstitch and the whiskers with French knots as shown on page 10 (Photo 10).

Photo 10

18. Position a standard segment, the head, a standard segment and the tail clockwise in a circle (Photo 11). **Note:** *The tail is on the upper portion of the segment.* Using buttonhole twist thread and following the instructions for Forming Puzzle Ball Rings on page 9, stitch the four segments of the ring together.

Photo 11

19. Interlock the three rings referring to Assembling the Puzzle Ball on page 11 to create your lion puzzle ball. ●

Templates

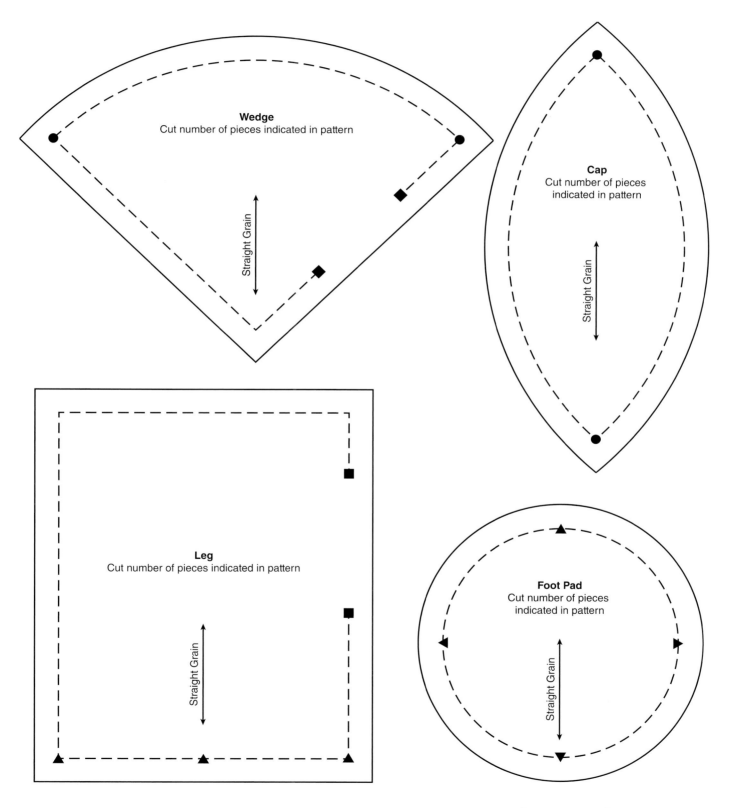

Wedge
Cut number of pieces indicated in pattern

Straight Grain

Cap
Cut number of pieces indicated in pattern

Straight Grain

Leg
Cut number of pieces indicated in pattern

Straight Grain

Foot Pad
Cut number of pieces indicated in pattern

Straight Grain

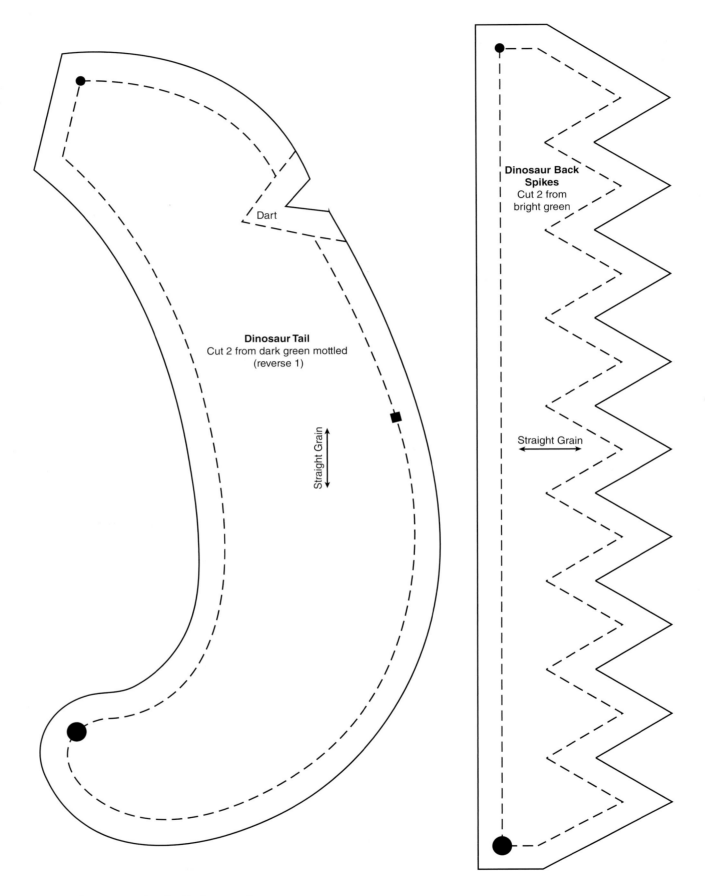

Dart

Dinosaur Tail
Cut 2 from dark green mottled
(reverse 1)

Straight Grain

**Dinosaur Back
Spikes**
Cut 2 from
bright green

Straight Grain

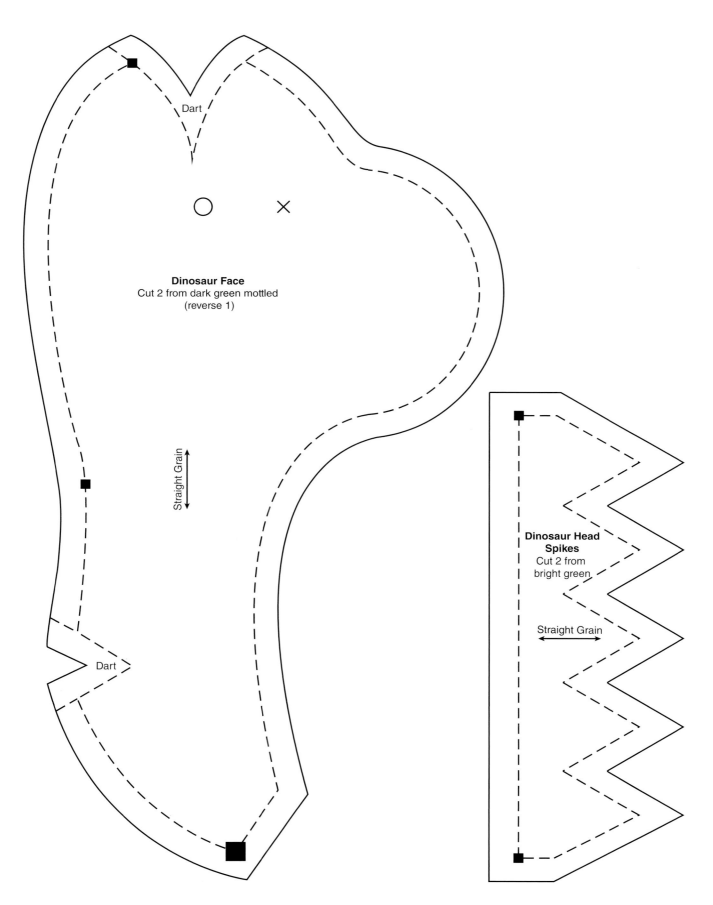

Dart

Dinosaur Face
Cut 2 from dark green mottled
(reverse 1)

Straight Grain

Dart

**Dinosaur Head
Spikes**
Cut 2 from
bright green

Straight Grain

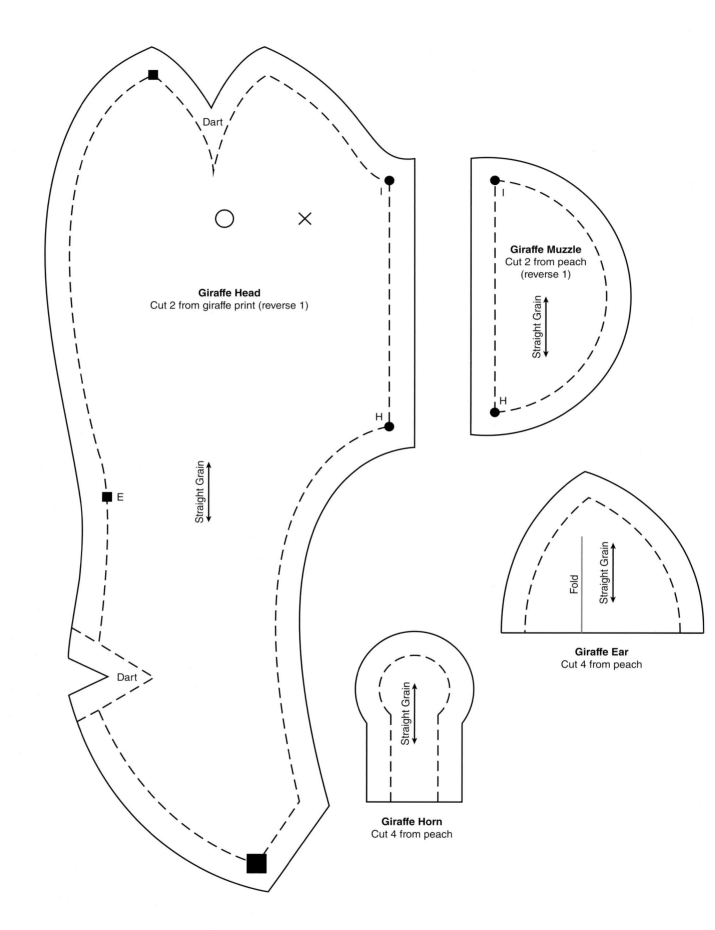

Giraffe Head
Cut 2 from giraffe print (reverse 1)

Dart

E

Straight Grain

H

Dart

Giraffe Muzzle
Cut 2 from peach
(reverse 1)

Straight Grain

I

H

Fold

Straight Grain

Giraffe Ear
Cut 4 from peach

Straight Grain

Giraffe Horn
Cut 4 from peach

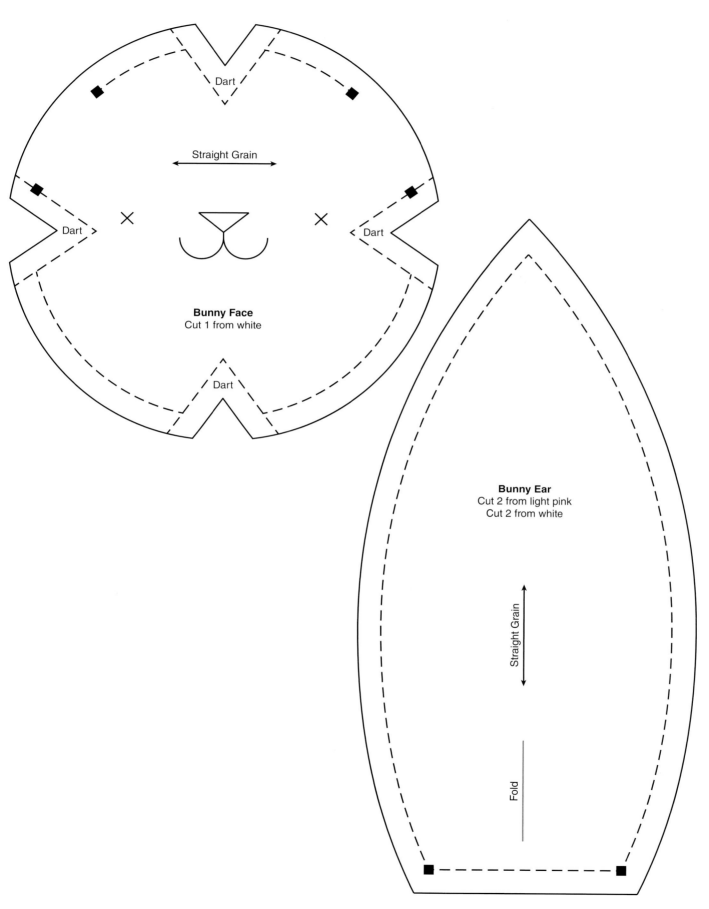

Bunny Face
Cut 1 from white

Dart

Dart

Dart

Dart

Straight Grain

Bunny Ear
Cut 2 from light pink
Cut 2 from white

Straight Grain

Fold

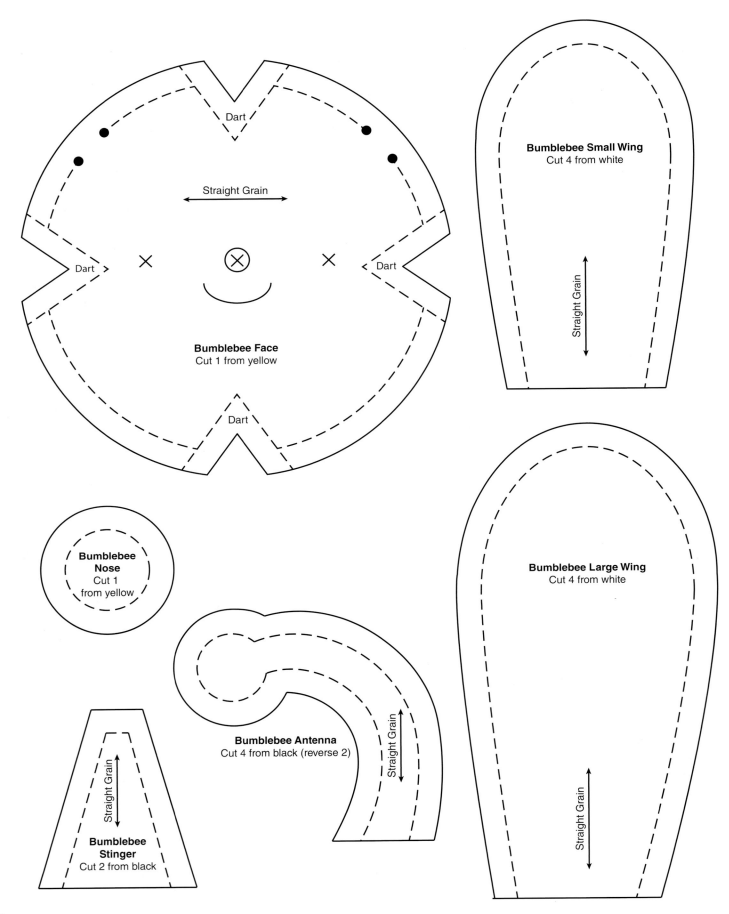

Bumblebee Face
Cut 1 from yellow

Straight Grain

Dart

Dart

Dart

Bumblebee Small Wing
Cut 4 from white

Straight Grain

Bumblebee Nose
Cut 1
from yellow

Bumblebee Large Wing
Cut 4 from white

Straight Grain

Straight Grain

Bumblebee Antenna
Cut 4 from black (reverse 2)

Straight Grain

Bumblebee Stinger
Cut 2 from black

Straight Grain